About the Author

Kelonie Utley resides in a small farming community in West Virginia with her family. Kelonie is currently a student at Berklee College of Music Online getting her bachelor's degree. Growing up, Kelonie battled with being abused and bullied. She began to open up through her gothic horror poetry that told the tales of her life story. She has been writing since she was seven years old and kept her writing secret for many years. In 2015, she broke her silence and started sharing her poetry with others going through hard times. Kelonie enjoys spending time with her family.

Altered Reality
Long Walk to Freedom

Kelonie Utley

Altered Reality
Long Walk to Freedom

Olympia Publishers
London

www.olympiapublishers.com
OLYMPIA PAPERBACK EDITION

A CIP catalogue record for this title is
available from the British Library.

ISBN: 978-1-78830-722-2

This is a work of fiction.
Names, characters, places and incidents originate from the writer's
imagination. Any resemblance to actual persons, living or dead, is
purely coincidental.

First Published in 2020

Olympia Publishers
Tallis House
2 Tallis Street
London
EC4Y 0AB

Printed in Great Britain

Dedication

Special dedication to Wesley Harmuth — I will always remember our special times watching cartoons together and the amazing letters shared. You are loved and missed dearly.
To Berklee College of Music staff and students, for believing in me and giving me a chance to shine.

Acknowledgements

Thank you to my family, the Shields family, Chris and Tim Grover, Mick C., April and Jurgen E.

Untold Stories

Memories, we all have them
Silenced we have made them
Walking as our own ghost
Hiding behind sheets
Afraid to share
What could break us.

Lies, we have all told them
Short stories turned to long ones
Words shared that weren't meant
Sewed teeth afraid to speak
To makes our lies into truth.

Sadness, we have all felt
Tears pouring inside like rain
Breaking us apart to shed new
Wars of pain scared to show
If only we could let us heal.

Love, we have all shared
Hands in hand, hearts as one
Bringing us closer to perfect.

Together we are sharing
Maybe if shared to the world
Our world could be whole.

Stories, we all have one
Life we have all lived
Life we're getting ready for
Yet we keep our life untold
Life stories left behind
Why can't we just share?

Maybe just
Maybe
A life can be saved.

Secrets

Waking up hearing your voice
Hearing every little word
Every little detail that makes me sad
Wishing I could change everything
Everything about you.

Laying around not wanting to see
I already heard how you feel
What have I done to get you?
I am just kept silent
'Cause I am only a lie.

I spend my days with you
When you never wanted me
I wiped your tears, hugged your heart
Just for you to accept me,
To only be pushed a side.

If people could only see
Could see the secrets you hid

Making you look great
I was seen as nothing
Behind the closed doors of you.

Remember secrets aren't forever
Blood one day of you will shed
Truths will bleed setting me free
Free of all the secrets
Secrets you kept to save you.

I lived beneath you for so long
Now I am free from you
I live sharing your secrets
I will never be ashamed
I'm forever real
Keeping no secrets.

Crypts of Time

Bind me into chains
Stone walls filled with sadness
Lingering in images
Of memories long gone
Striking me into darkness.

Holding back in rust
Watching taunting shadows
Fighting within my head
Locked into bars of eyes
Not able to break free
From the darkness within me.

Feeling pain of inner
passion Laying within desire
Watching closed curtains
Hiding my demons from within
Afraid of darkness.

Waking lost in time
Fears devouring the night

Stones turn to dust
Baring inner thoughts
Decaying within my mind
As the darkness takes hold of me.

Red and Black Wires

Running through my own spectrum of colors
Trying to be careful not to blend with any other.
Hiding in my own connection of red and black wires,
Which keeps me together from falling apart.

Always covering up everything inside that makes me
whole.
Afraid to show all others how I truly bleed, for I am like
no other.
I stand alone stuck in a maze of red and black wires,
Making me fragile to the world around me.

Wires flow through me like veins
Keeping my mind afloat
Holding together to breathe another day,
Shall my wires break,
Life I see before me fades away.

My destiny lays within my wires, locking me up,
Hiding myself from what I cannot see.
Wires I keep adding to lock into me,

Making me see through, so no one can see me.
Nor save me from being a face lost in time.

Closing my eyes as I crawl back into my corner of dead
images.
Blending into my own spectrum of colors hiding me
from you
Therefore, recreating more red and black wires to bind
me from all I can feel in me.

Falling in the Eyes of Evil

Wars of hate fall upon
Streets ridden of pain
Forgotten ones run away
Alone on broken stones
Tears of hate break free.

A life faded into darkness
Punches take their toll
Bruises appear showing truth
Building into a storm.

End the wars of silence
Inside of me
From falling in eyes of evil.

Pacing my inner dark halls
A mind created from hate
Time can only fade the wars of pain
Yet another falls
In the hands of evil.

Scars of battle
Shows its design
Mirrors of the broken
Staring into madness
Caving under pressure
Of one more hit.

Knees bent
Hands folded too above
Take my pain away
Keep me from falling
In eyes of evil.

Altered Reality

Our visions lost within
Tears of hate fall from you
Eyes close to what was old, shedding the new
Afraid of the feeling of darkness turning to light
Thy mind falls into pieces
To what I cannot see.

Lies within thy truths, truths within false views
Lying dormant in fears
I shall cry no more within an altered reality.

Minds of new, bring pain of old
World crashing on me as one
Mazes close in to see the path ahead
I fall on bended knees.

Fight away this need, fight away this fear
I stand alone in a mind of altered lies
Storms brew behind thy eyes
Bursting into flames
I fight away this need, fighting away this fear.

Away I fly into a mind of nothing
Hiding my paths into me
Following what I cannot lead
I fall behind
In the false beliefs of others
in an altered reality.

Fight away this need, fight away this fear
I stand alone in a mind of altered lies
Storms brew behind thy eyes
Bursting into flames
I fight away this need, fighting away this fear.

Thy shall fall, thy shall perish
In this world of visions
We see no truth
I shall fall away in this altered reality.

Less Than Me

Thy days fall behind fallen eyes
Tears of my hope
Shy away in me
Losing me to what I was
To what can't be seen.
I love with my hardest
I die in you.

Only we can see
What we could be
You shy into the storms of pain
I hide within shadows
I will never be
But less than me.

Thy heart falls on hard days
Hope faded into what can't be seen
I walk alone
In my forest of tears
Forever dying inside
For what I can never be.

Hate fills my eyes
You looking back at me in lies
seeing myself becoming
less than me.

Words spoken
Words lost within time
Going astray from broken promises
I hide in my shame
As I fall back to
Being less than me.

Only in Time

The dawn is coming.
My wickedness is fading
Time is running from me
Am I mad, they say?
Am I lost they say?
Who knows, but me?
Hurry, free me from this spell.

Come feel my magic
Before the dawn of time
Just a wish, just one
It is all I need
They then can set me free
Free from dying in my storm.

Oh, the madness, oh the strain
Oh my.
Oh no
My dawn is almost near
This dust you hold
Shall slumber with me

As you see, time can only tell
Set me free or forever lost I'll be
Burning in time upon the dawn.

Oh, please do come back
Only at night I shall live
I shall feed you all my lies
In my dust of magic
You will think;
Are you mad?
Are you lost?
Only I shall know
'Cause only I can give the time.

Don't Wanna Cry No More

Her tears are flowing like a river
Sitting there drowning in a thought
Words replaying over
Her mind starts drifting apart.

She cries out in anger
With others bringing her down
Judging her, hating her
She just falls to the ground
And wonders
Should I just drown?

Don't
Don't wanna cry no more
I don't wanna hate no more
Please come rescue me
I can't take me
Any more.

Should she lose this thought
Shall she silence this pain

With a bang to my head
Would it make peace in me?

Silent wars are winning
Words of others cutting her down
Judging her,
Hating her
She just can't handle herself
And wonders
Should I just drown.

When I'm too far gone
Will my story be told?
Will anyone notice
I am forever gone?

Don't wanna cry over me no more.

Imprisoned Mind

If thy eyes wake to the morning mists
Will I see the fog of the roaming
souls?

Soiled truths lost in thee
altered reality. Beliefs spilling ruins
of my prison wars
Lost inside the tomb of stones forgotten
Three words spoken fall to lies of weary.
Held tight in thee burnt tales of my pain.
Thy doors lock forever in faltered gates.

If thy eyes close in the dreary night
Will I see the path to thy mindless crypt?
Thy lies flowing into reddened glass veins
A broken mind set free of thy horned chains
My soul sets fire letting go of false wings.

If thy eyes see in a new fading light
Will I see the walls of stone to thy heart?
Broken within the beats of thy time

Beating to thee song of no sound
Where pain is swollen in thy hunger
Thy forever holding thee story
I forever try to shed for thee.

Silent Voices

She's only another face in the crowd
Another face in a school system of hate
Always walking alone with her head held low
Feeling every evil stare, hearing every word
That is breaking her into pieces
Only she knows her mind
Feeling alone hearing silent voices.

In her mind she screams,
Why can't they see, can't they see?
See what is building inside of me
Damn, I can't control what they are
Doing to me.

All these fears these kids put in me
Their words that are turning circles
Circles in my head,
In my head
They're in my head filling me
With their poisoned lies
Don't they see what is building

Building inside of me
Hearing these silent voices screaming in my head
Unwanted anger, anger they've built in me
Their words that are torturing me
In my mind I hear silent voices
That I can't control.

At home she doesn't show her pain
Living life as if things were all okay
Her parents don't have a clue, to what
To what is brewing inside of her
They only know the smiles she fakes
As she heads to school hating herself.

All she can hear is silent voices beating at her
Inside she cries, afraid of what she will do
So, she hides in her corner, building up her war
One more look around this school
She finally breaks.

Falling to floor she screams
Please save me from me
Doesn't anyone hear
Hear what is building in me
All these voices,
Damn the voices
Building inside of me
Hearing these silent voices screaming in my head
Unwanted anger, anger they've built in me
Their words that are torturing me
In my mind I hear silent voices

That I can't control.

She is only another face
Another face remembering
Past words of hate.

Psycho Words

There she was staring at me,
A beauty
Catching my sight, catching my heart
She engulfed me in her ways
I was trapped within her net
Oh, how perfect it felt
With her and I.

Her words stabbing my every breath
There she went breaking me
For what I gave her wasn't good enough
Happy moments erased with pain.

Your sweet little psycho words
Built me so
High and mighty
Just to feel what I couldn't keep
Words I held so dear and true
Were only pieces of your glass
Cutting me in two.

Yeah, your little psycho words
Seemed so sweet
Stabbing me.

Every smile you created, destroyed
The smiles turned upside down
Questioning my every breath
If only my heart could
Fade the memory of you.

This whole time she made me
Doubt me, doubt my worth
She thought she could break me.

How wrong you are
dear Look at me now living life
I have moved on from you
No more of your sweet little psycho words
Because I am going to love me
And I know love will find me
Thanks to you I am alive.

Wars of you

I long for a day without my war
A day without the fighting in my head
Hating the fact, I can't let the past be
Everywhere I look your smirking
Seeing your memory looking back at me.

I never could stand up to you when you had breath
Yet I still can't stand up to what you have turned me
into
Even though you have faded out
You haunt every memory
I live on dead inside because of the war you have built
in me.

Wish for once you'd just let me breathe
To accept the person in me
You have blinded me to happiness
Locking me into a battle I can't win.

For now, I am closed because of you
To never believe in me.

All you cared about was you
If only you had half the heart
Everyone thought you once had.

In a way I am just like
you I hide from my past
Hiding in the shadows from all who try to love me
Because of you, I lay broken in my mind
Confused to what to accept in me.

I have longed for a day
Where I never have to think of you
A day without a memory of you
Yet everywhere I look
You're standing there taunting me
Starring back at me, laughing because I am broken.

In my dreams, you're making me cry out in pain
Like you have always done
Pulling my hair
Grabbing my head to try to erase
Myself away from you
Wondering when I can let go of what I never had.

My past makes me weak
Constantly scared it will repeat itself
Afraid of the tears of pain that could fall once more
Because of you, I fall each day
Tired of falling away from trust
Being sacred to ever love with the fears you built in me.

I close myself up
Screaming in despair of demons you made dance in my
head
Why can't you just let me be?
To a future I could possibly change
A future where happiness can dance in colors
Sharing love that you were never able to give.

I head back to my dark corners crying
Where you always left me
A grown woman trapped in a child's face full of fears
Looking for an escape to be saved from you.

In my shadows
You can't hurt what is already hurting
I lay back in my mind
Smothering me from past memories
Of wondering why
Am I still afraid of you?

Leaving me behind

Thoughts running away in my mind
Hoping your words to be true
With false smiles on my lips
I hide my true feelings for you
Watching you walk away
Leaving me behind.

Looking in my broken mirror
Wondering what is wrong with me
Staring into shattered glass
I notice my lines forming
Thinking maybe my face is a tale
To why you're leaving me behind.

Hearing your words
Therefore, I fall into your embrace
Your warmth is my glow
Yet you grow cold
Keeping me lost in lies
Seeing you leaving me behind.

Believing in a dream
I stand by you
Withering away from me
Tears fall like sand
Knowing I can never have you
Sitting in silence
As you leave me behind.

You see my tears
As clear as day
Happiness fading fast each day
Knowing what needs to be done
Turning away
Taking hurtful steps further away
Daring to not look back
Growing accustomed to the ways
I walk away leaving us behind.

Better in Me

Stars shining in night skies
Dancing around me
Truth within life
Falls on me.

Broken in ways of beauty
Visions of love fill in me
Striving to be me.

Pictures of memories
Of who I want to be
Fighting to take a hold of me.

Crying for time
Guiding me
To want to be a better me.

Smiles within light
Winds of happiness
Ignites in me.

Journeys of a new
Helping me
On a path
To a better me.

My Disease

Roaming in darkness
Awaiting the hunger
Hiding away in silence
Finding you lingering
Trying to catch a glimpse of me
The smell of your flesh
Feels the air with sweet aroma
Night chills take me over
As my disease flourishes.

Watching you pass
With your sword held high
Slowly following
In your steps of desire
Hungry for your touch once more
Emotions filling within me
Spiraling out of control
My disease is what beats in you.

Grabbing a hold
Staring into cold eyes
Skin so warm

Against my decaying soul
Lusting for your love
Shedding my blood rotted tears
For one I cannot claim
My disease is you.

Letting you go
Seeing your sword sway
I feel no more
Screams of hunger gone silent
To a pain long gone
My disease is still alive within
The memories of us.

Once loved in life
By a heart
so strong Yet in death
I'm lost within you
Lying wondering in a time passed
A fear of what I have become
Within my disease.

You might think I am gone
Remember my cold heart still beats
Till next time
You fall on me
For always I will haunt your dreams
With the disease of me.

Voices of War

Confusion of worlds set fire
Leading us to shadowed illusions
Losing within a mind maze
With the voices of war.

Paths of the chosen
Ruled in chains
Worlds fall to destruction
Tears of false needs turn to
Screams of the unknown
Neighbors devour our souls.

Hiding within colors
Restricted to be heard
We march to be free
From hands of pain.

Wars of belief
Have taken the toll
On what we used to be
To being told

What we will be.

Presence of life gone
Bombs bring darkness
Turning skies in acid
Mutated from the
Voices of war.

Distant Whispers

Walking alone in coldness
Hiding away in fear
Falling into darkness
Crumbling into ash
Winds come through
Spreading ashes to make me whole
Gentle hands recreate a new
No longer fearing
love I start my journey
Leading me to distant whispers.

Closing my eyes
Letting my tears fall for you
My heart becomes one with yours
Leaves of color dancing around us
Feeling happiness
Of visions of you
Words of love spreading
Through me
Feeling distant whispers from you.

Spreading my wings
Seeing my beauty grow within
Rain falls down on me
Showering me in love
Smiling at tender
touches I fall deep within you
Hearing your distant whispers.

Faces life in a new light
A path opens to you
Eyes filled with passion
Soaring within us
Bringing you into me
Feeling your pleasure
Rebuilding broken glass
Melting in your love for me
Through our distant whispers.

Intertwined

Night glazes over head
Angels lay their weary heads
Closing to the world around
Falling into dreamful slumber
Soaring through darkness
To intertwine in love.

Dark hearts at rest
Upon their clouds of dreams
Showering tears of love
Holding on for a chance
To be whole with you
Intertwined in the arms of love.

Wings spread open
Waiting for bodies to unite
Making us one in life
Feeling your poison
Eating at my very desires
Intertwined in love with you.

Bodies of the night heat
Making flames of passion
Burning our love
Forever indented in our skin
We form as one
As we are intertwined in love.

Vampiric Desires

Searching worlds on end
Soaring in the skies
Finding my forever lost soul
Wondering among in the mist of shadows
Peeking out through clouds of red
Longing to find my stolen heart
For which I shall desire.

In our worlds apart
You come forth
My inner being growing
Becoming whole in the presence
Searching for a long-waited desire
Which stands before me.

A desire of strength
Hearts combined into one
Flesh heated with blood
As desires pour over me
Lust mixing as one
A true being has formed.

A love so powerful
To defeat against all odds
Visions of you come ashore
Once held in dreams
Has become reality
As a stand against time.

Awaiting the day
To sink the teeth
Into the warm flesh of love
Bodies come together
Yearning for pleasure
Two souls into one
Colliding into ash
Holding on
From one desire to the next.

A life without a heart
A life faded in shadows
A heart beat just for you.

A fight I hold to the end
Spending my last breath
For a dance of eternity
With you.

Desires for only one
A guardian of darkness takes hold
Awaiting each world for you
A desire is a journey

The journey is our love.

Living as one in darkness
In worlds apart
Faith of a heart never ending
I hunger of your blood
As you hunger for mine.

My sweet desires gain strength
Living forever
In my womb of Vampiric desires.

Anyone Like You

Fears of night
Falling into day
Lost in words of others
I discover myself in you
Falling away from hate
Your touch brings me into love.

Eyes lost within silence
Words of you touch my skin
Falling into you
Once alone, laying broken
You piece me together
Bringing me breath.

Oh, what I do for your kiss, your touch,
Your smile falling in my eyes
Melting two hearts as one
Falling deeper in you
What I'd give for
Anyone like you.

In your embrace
Becoming whole
My inner beauty dancing
Within your stares
Watching me
Come to life.

Opening my eyes
To what I could never see
You touch me
Feeling me with your warmth
Giving me strength
Lift my desires to the stars.

As one we grow
Stronger in love
With hearts of touch
We live forever as one
In love.

When You're Gone

My skies grow weary
Wondering where you are
Losing myself within your presence
My heart only lives feeling you touching me
Daydreaming of your words you say to me
I live when you are with me
Your presence making me grow strong.

When you're gone
My heart falls
Waiting for your next touch
Awaiting the words to bring me home
Back into you
When you're gone
I die inside waiting for your love.

Sitting here saying difficult things
Getting your attention
Making you want me more
Falling in deeper
Entwined in me.

You never give up on me
Now our journey starts anew
I'm learning to love all over again
Trusting my heart in you
Praying for our day to be one.

You are my air, my eyes
When I can't breathe nor see
I struggle falling in love with you
Afraid of how beautiful touch will be
Never leave me alone without you.

My heart fades away for you
When you are so far from me
I am scared of your strength
Yet I'm falling deeper for you
My heart is now in your hands
That I am handing over to you.
When you're gone from me
I am nothing but an empty shell.

Feel Me Inside

When the light fades
Behind those clouds
Tears seem to never give way
Just look above
And I will shine my love on you.

Hands we held
Songs we sung
Will hold true to your heart.
I may be gone
But my heart will live in you.

Never back down
My dear child
I'm playing in heaven for you.
As you sing our song
Feel me inside.

Remember me
Your dark skies will clear
The path before you

Will be a lesson, in time.
Songs of old will come alive
Once more for you.

I may no longer walk
I'm still there standing with
you I'm alive in you.

Weeping Waters

Pretty little angels
Leaning over soiled waters
Smiling at the future
Shining through rapid weeping waters.

Pretty little fingers
Gliding fingers though the tears
Letting beautiful souls
Fly away home
Giving hope to those lost in time
In the weeping waters.

Little bits of beautiful laughter
Sprinkling glitter around all in sadness
Smiling at the darkness fading away in
Our weeping waters.

Little wings spread wide open
Catching us from falling into fear
Holding us high
To spread our wings of joy

We take flight in the heavens above
From the little angels
In our weeping waters.

Rivers of Red

Waters once flowing free
Glistening in a light blue gown
Dancing in waves of a fall breeze
A song of nature flowing
Between the rocks of love.

Creating life beneath the trees
Hearing the sounds
of birds Singing to one another
Leaves falling like rain,
Laying softly among the sheets.

Tears of beauty start growing
Alongside the river bed
Flowers of colors start breathing
Painting a picture of peace
Among an aging river.

Waters once of blue
Turning to the times of red
Baring the soil of created life

Fading new to age
Showing lines of wisdom.

Have now been laid to rest
In remembrance of a journey
That a river once lived
Rivers of red open new life
Creating new paths
Spreading free flowing waters.

Asylum

I am headed back into time
Roaming old torn walls of dread
Watching old films of black and white
Trying to fade back to innocence
Dancing in the windows of time.

These doors of past
Screams from my soul
Lying awake haunting me
Crying in fear of fresh air
Staying locked in a shadow
Inside my mental asylum.

In this mind of mine
I am feeling of a fading mist
Lingering to remember pictures
I would love to forget
Oh, how these walls shed the dirt
Falling down on me.

My own foot prints stained

On these old wooden floors
Hearing every creak
Taking me back in time
Remembering the abuse
Behind these asylum walls.

This house isn't a home
Just the death of my dreams
Murdered behind the walls
Of the punches I endured
I leave this asylum of my pain.

I will never look back
This road will not be taken
I will finally let go
Choosing to live
Breaking myself free from this asylum.

Changing My Direction

My winds are changing courses
Once so happy in a small family town
Back way down in the hills of beauty
We started to raise our family.
The times have faded
I learned the lies of love in a small town.

He was only a ghost pretending
I was just a shadow that followed behind
You made me doubt every breath
Made me doubt what love is
So now I have to move on
'Cause.

I am changing my direction
I won't let you cut me down
I refuse to live in your hell
Just because
You can't like yourself.
So, I am gone
Changing my direction

At one time, I saw you and I
Growing old in a small family town
But your lies never went through
You planned on leaving me a long time ago.

Well I am making it easier for you.
I am leaving you behind,
As a ghost you are pretending
To love through your lies
I won't hate me like you taught me too
'Cause I am moving on
Changing..

I am changing my direction
I won't let you cut me down
I refuse to live in your hell
Just because
You can't like yourself
So, I am gone
Changing my direction
How do you feel now?
Living alone with yourself
No one to love you,
No one for you to cut down
Now your nothing but an empty ghost
In a small forgotten town.

Where the Heart Echoes

She once walked in circles in his arms
Following every word of demands
Making her hide every vision.
She falls out of his false love to
Only write a new tale to hopefully
Soar away from his embrace.

Walking away from all his rules
Made it hard to believe in her
She ran from all the beautiful music
Ignoring her heart that echoes
To fly above the canyons,
With her pride she fights to build.

No longer missing his loving hate
On top of the world, not afraid to fall
Arms spread open with tears of
Freedom to hear happy sounds
For which was hidden so long
She smiles in love, letting
Her heart echo with dreams.

Her old heart is singing to a whole new tune.
Sad songs don't break her in two like they used too
She is hearing the echoes of a sweet surrender
Oh boy how she has grown
She stands upon her canyon alone
Yet in love to a whole new tune
This is where the heart echoes.

I was feeling beautiful

Met you while I was passing through town.
That smile just turned my world
Sent these chills down my spine
Making me smile with a blush
Then it became me and you
Starting a family of our own
I was feeling so beautiful.

The days came and went like a fog
Smiles we once shared tuned upside down
I was dressing up in your favorite dress
Just looking so beautiful for you
You didn't even notice me wanting you
I am only a ghost you don't want any more.

I was feeling so beautiful
Till your love faded from your heart.
Sitting next to you, watching you
Flirting with all those girls
Asking me, "Why can't you look like that?"

Now I'm sitting with tears feeling so ugly
Till my little boy came to me
"Mommy, please wipe your tears
You are so beautiful to me."
With his hugs and kiss.

I am feeling so beautiful with tears
Sitting next to my son
Wearing his favorite green dress
Smiles started glowing,
What a perfect day
To have the love of a little angel.

I met you while I was passing through
You smiled with a shine in your eye
That sent those chills down my spine
Then it became you and I
With a son by our side
Days came and went
Our love only grew stronger
You became his dad
Telling him,
"Look how beautiful your mom looks tonight."
I am feeling so beautiful.

I've Been Feeling Lonely

I was just sitting here thinking
Thinking under the blue skies
Letting the clouds take me
Take me to a lonely place
A lonely place missing you
I am just missing you.

All this thinking, thinking
Can't take you out of here
All the thinking
Has driven me crazy
Crazy, to the point
I've been feeling lonely.

I been feeling lonely
Yeah, I am just sitting here
Thinking, I am thinking
About you, about me
Maybe we're becoming more.

I was only thinking, thinking
Then you came

in like the rain
Sprinkling down upon me
Now I can't shed you
And I know I don't want too.

All this thinking, thinking
Can't take you out of here
All the thinking
Has driven me in love.
Isn't it crazy?
Crazy, I had been feeling lonely.

I been feeling lonely
Feeling lonely,
When you aren't around
I didn't think pain could
Be so beautiful, beautiful
Falling for you.

Make You Love Me

All I ever needed was this old dusty blue
guitar Roaming alone down these dirt end
roads Playing alongside a river bed
Not worried about a thing.

Just me and the beauty of Mother Nature
Feeling her touch through the breeze
Acting like this is the only thing I need
Roaming as a lonely musician
With not a care.

Then there came you
Racing through like the winds
Changing my mind, watching you
Making me rethink my old ways
Wondering could there be more?
Thank this old worn out guitar.

I came on you walking down this dirt end road
Watching you holding your red burnt guitar
Yet you didn't pay me any mind

You just passed me on by.

It was just me and Mother Nature
Yet I can only see you playing your guitar
Down by the side of this old river
But you were nowhere to be found.

Then there came you
Racing through like the winds
Changing my mind watching you
Making me rethink my old ways
Wondering could there be more?
Thank this old, worn out guitar.

Sitting down by the river watching the river flow
Leaves falling like dancing lovers under a country sky
I heard you playing a tune I know so well.
Grabbing my guitar, I started playing our tune
I just knew I was going to make you love me.

I saw that smile come my way
Then you got up and walked over to me
That was all it took to change my mind.
I am sitting next to you playing our song.

Then there came you
Racing through like the winds
Changing my mind, watching you
Making me rethink my old ways
Wondering could there be more?
Thank this old worn out guitar.

Here we still are twenty years later
Playing guitar, together, in love
Along with our little country family.

Porcelain Snow

Tiptoe, Tiptoe
In the porcelain snow
I was my parents' mistake
I cried to be loved, cried to be
Noticed, yet I was broken
Laying in silence in my own tears
Drowning from a love
That never came my way.

Growing, Growing
Into this glass doll
Afraid to hug, afraid to show them me
Standing afraid that I will break, but
This doesn't have to be me
I know I can make a change to be
Everything I want to be.

Tiptoe, Tiptoe
Back into a time where I was
Crying, screaming my winter storm
Quietly sneaking through the

Porcelain snow.

Behind my shattered ice window
Watching clouds frozen passing me
By tears of my eyes cracking
Turning pale gray standing still
Fading into the shadows of my ghost
Where they can't see me.

I was my parent's only mistake
Now look at me growing
Dancing, running in my glass globe
Straying away from broken
Broken love, broken promises
Growing as a child of blue.

Tiptoe, Tiptoe
Into my future where I
know I can make a change and
Be who I always wanted to be
Dancing freely underneath
The beautiful porcelain snow.

CPSIA information can be obtained
at www.ICGtesting.com
Printed in the USA
FSHW011629010820
72463FS